doubters and

dreamers

Volume 67

Sun Tracks
An American Indian Literary Series

Series Editor
Ofelia Zepeda

Editorial Committee
Larry Evers
Joy Harjo
Geary Hobson
N. Scott Momaday
Irvin Morris
Simon J. Ortiz
Kate Shanley
Leslie Marmon Silko
Luci Tapahonso

doubters and dreamers

Janice Gould

THE UNIVERSITY OF ARIZONA PRESS | TUCSON

The University of Arizona Press
© 2011 Janice Gould

www.uapress.arizona.edu

Library of Congress Cataloging-in-Publication Data
appear on the last printed page of this book.

Publication of this book is made possible in part by the proceeds of a
permanent endowment created with the assistance of a Challenge Grant
from the National Endowment for the Humanities, a federal agency.

Manufactured in the United States of America on acid-free, archival-
quality paper containing a minimum of 30% post-consumer waste and
processed chlorine free.

16   15   14   13   12   11   6   5   4   3   2   1

For Marie-Elise Wheatwind

For my sisters

And in memory of my father

contents

Tribal History

Indian Mascot, 1959

Now begins the festival and rivalry of late fall,
the weird debauch and daring debacle
of frat-boy parties as students parade foggy streets in mock
processions, bearing on shoulders scrawny effigies of dead,
defeated Indians cut from trees, where,
in the twilight, they had earlier been hung.

"Just dummies," laughs our dad, "Red Indians hung
or burned—it's only in jest." Every fall
brings the Big Game against Stanford, where
young scholars let off steam before the debacle
they may face of failed exams. "You're dead
wrong," he says to Mom. "They don't mock

real, live Indians." Around UC campus, mock
lynchings go on. Beneath porches we see hung
the scarecrow Natives with fake long braids, dead
from the merrymaking. On Bancroft Way, one has fallen
indecorously to a lawn, a symbol of the debacle
that happened three generations ago in California's hills, where

Native peoples were strung up. (A way of having fun? Where
did they go, those Indian ghosts?) "Their kids perform mock
war dances, whooping, re-enacting scenes of a debacle
white folks let loose," chides Mom. "Meanwhile we hang

portraits of presidents on school walls and never let fall
the old red, white, and blue. My dear brother is dead

because he fought in a White man's war. How many dead
Indians do they need to feel okay? This whole thing wears
on my soul." In the dark car we go silent, and the fall
night gets chillier. In yards, blazing bonfires mock
the stars that glow palely somewhere above. A thin moon hangs
over the tule fogs. I've never heard the word "debacle"

before and wonder what it means. "What's a debacle,
Mom?" I ask. "Oh, honey, it's a terrible and deadly
collapse. Complete ruin." I've noticed how the hung
Indians have their heads slumped forward. They wear
old clothes, headbands with feathers, face paint, moc-
casins instead of boots. Little do we know, this fall,

living Indians at Feather Falls
leave tobacco to mark that, indeed,
we're still here, lungs full of indigenous air.

Renegade

Mama was no reservation squaw. Abandoned
but not disowned, she married white and went back home
only when the tank was full, smoking at a steady fifty
up the river road, taking each snake-eyed turn in stride.

The town was nothing on a nowhere map, a wide space
on a sandbar, a one-horse resort lost among the mountains
no one named but Indians. We loved to own the road
in Mom's blue Ford, windows rolled down, hair flying loose,
brown feet on the plump back seat. Heat was our legacy:

willows bending in summer wind, stones sweltering in cliffs,
thin waterfalls plunging to their deaths. We laughed
and chortled with songs sacred to our people, Wee-mo-way
and Kumbaya, while Mom hummed other tunes recollected
from earlier wars—Green Grow the Lilacs, Strawberry Roan,
The Butcher Boy. At journey's end we knew

there'd be a pot of coffee, black and steamy,
even in the midday glare, and our mother's sister
chuckling while they talked and sucked that universal candy:
hard butterballs and marbles of cinnamon, wedges
of sugary orange. Sometimes they argued over stories
as they worked on another afghan or rag doll or lifted
flattened flowers from a fat catalog, the electric iron

sizzling on waxed paper that encased blue larkspur
and sticky Mimulus in gauzy cards that
mimicked the color of tule fog.

While my uncle dug weeds in his colossal garden,
we kids lolled on the couch swing or walked
far up the dusty road to gather sweet peas
in the evening dusk. I only wondered about ghosts
when darkness fell among the darkest trees,
only worried about floods when all the lights went out
and we could hear the adults
whispering guilty reminiscences,
or the river in its restless bed,
ancient waters covering our dead.

Tribal History

When I think of my mother's hands,
brown and square, fingers slightly bent
from years of work, I consider
all the other hands of Concow folk,
bound, prepared
for the lynching at the crooked oak
along the mountain road
near the town of Cherokee.
It stood not far from the meadows
where our ancestral people made their home.

This was in the time when white men
scoured those hills, breaking them
down into rubble in their crazy search
for gold. The treaty with the Concow
would not be ratified by Congress,
for Indians were in the way of "progress,"
and though a promise had been made
to provide corn starch and other commodities
to every man who made his X
on that scrap of parchment,
the only X the white men made
was to cross the hands of Indians
behind their backs before swinging them
out over the lava walls of the canyon.

We Could Not Forget

The journey began, and the soldiers trudged all around us
that fall they stole us from our homeland.
We had a great distance to cover.
We left everything, all that we held familiar.

That fall they stole us from our homeland,
having herded us into corrals for cattle.
We left everything, all that we held familiar—
the granite rocks of the canyon, the buckeye and laurel.

Having herded us into corrals for cattle,
the soldiers were nervous we'd escape and posted armed guards.
The granite rocks of the canyon, the buckeye and laurel
whispered prophetic stories we could not forget.

The soldiers were nervous we'd escape and posted armed guards.
They trained their guns on us. Just at sunrise the winds arose and
whispered fearful stories we could not forget.
In a storm of dust and tears we began our trek.

They trained their guns on us. Just at sunrise the winds arose and
warned us not to flee, not to resist.
In a storm of dust and tears we began our trek,
men, women, and children, angry and afraid. The soldiers

charged us not to flee, not to resist.
So we stumbled, tired, hungry, through valley heat,
men, women, and children. Angry and afraid, the soldiers
pushed us along, impatient with our tears.

So we stumbled, tired, hungry, through valley heat.
We had a great distance to cover.
Pushed along, impatient with our tears,
our journey began, and the soldiers trudged all around us.

Feather River Sonnets

1

They lease a cabin where the river bends.
The canyon's wider here but steep just north
where summer clouds have billowed in. He tends
a big garden on the flood plain, and Fourth

of July we visit them, Mom's sister
Lil and her husband Ivan, a three-pack
smoker, curmudgeon, a sour trickster
with a stubby thumb from his lumberjack

days. Lil sews, cooks, presses flowers, crochets
afghans, knits socks, cans fruit, and cleans. She carps
about the stifling summer heat and says
she lives too far away. "But if I harp,

he'll take me to Smorgy's," she winks and nods.
He soon comes in with carrots from their yard.

2

Sometimes a rattler slips into the grass
and creeps along with raised head and flicking
tongue. "Ivan, grab the dog and make it fast!"
Lil shouts. Our heavy uncle runs, ticking

off the yards in seconds to scoop the pup,
a Chihuahua named Itty-Bit, who snaps
and growls because my uncle will not let up
teasing him. (But he adores that dog, wraps

him in the crook of his arm, carries
him everywhere.) Ivan seizes a hoe
to behead the snake, and if we tarry
outside a moment, he will curse and throw

a rock to herd us away. Ruffian
of sorts, his words are gruff, his old face grim.

3

At the cabin relative peace prevails.
We hardly fight. No one yells, storms, or cries
or feels called upon to stretch the truth, lie,
or dissemble. Grades? Who cares? No one fails,

at least not much. We can dress like boys, no
one disapproves. This willful ignorance
is nice. We hike, fish, swim, run. Kick the Can's
our favorite game. We watch the river flow,

pick gold poppies on the road, listen to
the wind that blows each afternoon. Our mom
seems merry away from home and Dad, from
worries about money, about him, who

does what dads do without family near—
funny things, perverse, all a little queer.

4

Our mom and aunt were born just down the road
when muleback was the customary mode
of transport. Goods came by train, and a stage-
coach ran from Innskip through red dust and sage

and dry manzanita. Things smelled of sweat,
leather, wool, coal, and smoke. People would get
letters written in ink by pens with brass
nibs. "Dearest Mother, just a line to ask

how you are doing, how are Cindy, Jacques,
Leander? Has Dad struck gold, did the flock
of ducks survive? Did your old cow give up
the ghost?" Fifty years later we feel rup-

tured from this past—almost. Our mom and aunt,
in tandem, laugh, "Bring back those times? You can't."

5

"Of course, the river's dammed up now," says Mom,
"and Jim Lee's pergola is gone. He tapped
the soda springs for tourists and mapped
a place for picnic lunches near our home.

Folks came by train and walked along the trail—
there was no highway then. Jim kept a stone
beneath his arm. The boys said, 'If he throws
that rock at your feet, you will die, frail

and consumptive.' We knew he had power,
practiced Indian cures. Strange things went on.
The spirit world was present. Now they're gone.
Remember the ceremony, the flowers

we picked when Mama died?" she asks Aunt Lil.
"Singing to that wild river?" Neither smile.

6

"The kids would never tell me what went on
in Indian school. I know that it burned down
is all. They came home scarred, hair full of lice.
Dad cut it short, and they used turpentine

to kill the bugs. It stung their scalps. They cried,
the girls did. 'If you get that in your eyes,
you'll go blind,' they said." Mom waits a spell,
then resumes. "They built another grade school

in Belden. The kids went there. They learned
to read, write, do math. They never felt spurned
by their classmates, and they liked their teacher.
I was young, but I'd have walked ten acres

to go to school, as little as I was," she cries,
fiery determination in her eyes.

7

We hike up Yellow Creek to Grandpa's claim,
an old abandoned mine, cabin with worn
planks, dynamite beneath the iron frame
of the bed. No gold now, only the torn

face of the cliff, wind in cedar and pine,
and the cold creek, numbingly cold and clear,
breaking over rocks, splashing us with fine
spray. Late in the afternoon a mule deer

comes down to drink from the glistening pool
by the boulders. Skinny water snake glides
past our legs, all brown speed and sleekness, fool-
ing us—it's not a twig. Day's heat subsides

much like Grandpa's dream of fat, easy wealth.
He died poor, a drunk, in consumptive health.

8

"Aunt Lil will not admit that he was cruel
when he drank. Our father would beat his sons
till the blood ran down their backs. The only one
he never hit was me. I was too small."

Mom sighs. We're seated at the river's edge
on a sandy bar in warm, bright sunshine.
I glance at her face. The dark, furrowed line
between her brows has deepened, a hard ledge

of memory. The river splashes by.
A tanager alights in the wind-whipped
willows. It flits yellow feathers.—We've dipped
our hands in water, prayed. We ever try

to appease what burns, what lacerates:
the loss of trust, ferocious tears, old hates.

9

"The boys all scattered when our mama died.
The girls found work in the city—housemaids.
Our dad shacked up with Annie Lee and stayed
drunk. Sister Bertha never liked the lights

and came back home to the mountains. She passed
away young." Mom's tales fill my tender heart.
West of us Mt. Ben Lomand stands, parts
white, puffy thunderheads that mount up fast

at canyon's rim. I know we Concow
have lived here a long time. Hunted and fished,
told stories, had ceremonies, had wished
to keep old ways and family ties, no doubt.

"But everything we loved," says Mom, "seems gone.
Earth and homestead, our tongue, our place, our songs."

10

Mom wakes us early. It's Monday. Full moon
in the canyon. Home to Berkeley, the bay,
ocean fog. We'll have eggs, toast. Pretty soon
we'll be on the road, silent and dismayed

at having to leave this place. I hate
good-byes, but the canyon shimmers in light
from the moon, and now that sad, longing ache
begins to wane. Granite looks slick at night

beneath the lunar glow. At eight we're home,
having sped down the two-lane delta road.
I know the river's back there—fine, red loam,
serpentine and mica rocks, the sunny load

of water, smell of sawmills, yellow pine.
Things I claim—though they never can be mine.

Discontent

We could hear her
knocking down strands of cobweb
from ceilings—sticky filaments,
sacs of eggs—as we woke most mornings
to a worm of discontent.
It lodged beneath the heart,
rubbed our frayed nerves,
gnawed at the gut, spleen,
ovaries. Filth

was Mom's first enemy, so each day
began with ritual cleaning: the stab
and sweep of the broom down the dark hall,
over the stained and scratched oak floors.

For weeks, she held her dust mop
one-handed, and with the other
cupped a hernia, while she swore
at us kids in that hard voice—a litany of our sins
and failures: sloth,
stupidity, secrecy.

We watched her
smash the spiders that ran, herky-jerky,
along the baseboards, while we ran, too.

Glaring at each other,
we gathered up the scattered
laundry, our father's shoes,
his newspapers and tools, our books,
drawings, music, sweatshirts,
and jackets, whatever
we'd left lying around.

We were guilty, but good
at evasion. We cultivated
shrewish or obsessive behaviors of our own: my tough
older sister sneered and stalked out of the house
to meet her boyfriend;
my sweet younger sister
trembled and cried, comforted
by one of our many dogs.
I slammed doors, pounded them
with my fists, screamed, "Shut up,
shut up, shut up!" She couldn't

leave us alone. She loved us
too much.

Though we were quick, she was
quicker. Her words stung.

We must have deserved it.

Flu, 1962

Shadows lengthened while we sat stuck in traffic just beyond San
Rafael. Headlights had begun to flare in the cool dusk. The hum of the
car's engine lulled me, and I put my forehead against the glass, looking
out over a darkening landscape. We were headed to the Bishop's Ranch,
a weekend retreat for Episcopal Young Churchmen in hilly country
that would someday produce superlative wines with garnet hues that
stain the inside of a glass. I was queasy from the lurching of the car,
the stops and starts, the smell of exhaust. Though trembling with cold,
I was too shy to ask the lady, the mother of one of the other girls,
to turn on the heater. I imagined pale pink blossoms on the Japanese
plum, apple trees laden with white flowers, and north of Sebastapol the
vibrant yellow of daffodils on slender, pleated stems. That night I slept
in a single bunk made up with thin sheets and blankets.

A warm sun the next day restored me, but in the evening, seated by
the fire that crackled in the fireplace of the big lodge, I felt flushed.
Our recently ordained curate (we were not to know he was gay till
some years later) had asked me to bring my guitar, and now he wanted
me to sing about the girl who decides to sleep next to her mother her
whole life long instead of falling for an unfaithful suitor. I sang; we
all sang together. Young Father W. had a wonderful tenor voice. His
smile reassured me, but now I was tired and, earlier than the others, I
decided to return to the dorm.

In that clear March night, the sky gleamed like black ink and stars
blazed, bright and alive. Walking downhill, guitar in hand, I suddenly

stumbled with dizziness, and the slope swam before me. "Hold on, hold on," I told myself as I nearly fell onto the dew-slick lawn. For a moment I could sense myself floating away from my body. Back in the dorm, I crawled into bed and lay shuddering with cold, bones aching. The room seemed to spin. I wanted to be home, but the thought of facing my mother filled me with terrible dismay. I knew the blue failure notice mailed by the school would have arrived.

Sure enough, it lay open on the dining table when I got home the following afternoon. A Sunday fog, hardly a mist, had blown in from the bay and was gathering in the eucalyptus across the ravine. The house was steamy. A basket of clean laundry occupied a chair atop a stack of San Francisco Chronicles. Mom sat at the table sewing, but I knew she was scowling. I thought it wise to look industrious, so I began to fold towels and pillowcases. "What I want to know," began my mother, "is whether you have any ambition? Obviously, you will never get to college. What do you expect to do with your life?" She paused, and I shrugged. "Go ahead and shrug. Do you think your girlfriend is going to take care of you? That won't last long. And why is it you only fall in love with girls? Well, I suppose you want to be a boy." What an unutterable failure I am. I retreated, burned by her ferocious, upright anger. "Oh, yes, I'm sure you're sick! But you will go to school tomorrow!"

That night, wracked again with cold, unable to stop my trembling, I sought my parents' bed, stood moaning till Mom woke and let me under the covers, where she tried to warm me with her body. Weeks later we learned that one of my classmates, a robust girl who shot baskets as well as any boy, had succumbed to the illness and died. That night, my mother placed her hand on my forehead—her smooth palm, her touch, gentle—and said to my barely awake dad, "Our daughter has a raging fever." Like a miracle, I was still her child. Comforted, I slept.

Für Elise

Why were they in tears
by the end of their lessons,
those red-faced young girls who,
right after school, arrived at our house
in their dresses or uniforms?
They trudged up the several steps,
sat on the squeaky piano bench,
placed their fingers on the keys,
and played "Für Elise," while Mom beat out the tempo with a wooden ruler.
I'd hear her counting, "One and two
and three and four. Read the notes!
Read the notes!" Mom whacked time
on a stack of loose music piled atop the piano,
a dark baby grand with massive
carved legs.

Poor girls. In the dining room
across the hall, I tied reeds
and scraped them down
with precise tools
for my oboe, practiced
the Marcello, Handel,
or Gluck. If I were bored,
I'd get out my guitar
and imagine myself

dressed in black,

accompanying Baez,

harmonizing on a folk tune.

Upstairs, my younger sister might

be practicing her flute.

Those afternoons, our house

hummed like a conservatory.

At dusk, I'd go to the kitchen,

start dinner—meatloaf or pot roast

with onions and potatoes. If they burned,

I would go out in the hall, open

the wide front door, evacuate

the smoke. Through the wavy glass

of the French doors, I could see Mom

standing above her student, a scorched look

on her face. She'd purse her lips and,

with her wrist, push back a shock

of thick, salty hair

that fell over her brow.

Those girls would never defy our mom

like we did, ignoring her demands

and requests, never deafen themselves

to the things that made her angry

and bitter. I couldn't help but feel

superior. Secretly I watched the child who,

hunched and red-faced, would stare mulishly at the music, hands

flat on the piano. Then she'd stumble

dutifully through the Beethoven,

over and over, tear-streaked,

humbled.

Off to the Music Lesson

Just beyond the steep hairpin turn on Del Mar Avenue, three blocks from home, my ankle twists on an edge of asphalt, and my right foot smashes against hard-packed soil. I stumble into a parked car; the oboe and my book of études go flying and land among the thistles. With the sudden ache in my foot, I break into a sweat. Should I return home? That would mean facing my mom's wrath. It would take twenty minutes to walk back up the hill, only to have her yell, "You came home because of a turned ankle? I pay good money for those lessons, and you haven't touched that instrument all week! So if you think I'm going to drive you because you're late, you're out of luck!" Leaning against the car, I remove my loafer, empty it of grit and pebbles, and gingerly dust off the instep of my bare foot against my left calf. I shut my eyes against the pain. I don't dare look at my foot, but slip it back in the shoe, then straighten my skirt and gather my book and the instrument from among the weeds. Clumping ahead, I try out different methods for walking without bearing down too much.

The steep road is shady beneath the eucalyptus along Glendale, but La Loma is bright with plum and apple blossoms and the forever view through the Golden Gate. On this Saturday afternoon, the bay looks steely beneath the pale sky. A pair of mourning doves perches cozily on the phone lines above the oblique walkway. I can smell the pungent fragrance of acacia trees. Beyond Buena Vista Road, I take the short-cut down the paved back steps of my old elementary school, Hillside, bracing myself against the iron rail. The air is moist beneath a canopy of lilacs and bare madrones. Reaching Hilgard, I wait to cross busy Euclid Avenue, then Scenic and Arch. Limping, I force my weight onto the metatarsus and my big toe. *It's not that bad*, I say aloud, but I don't quite believe it.

The streets are no longer precipitous, the grade hardly noticeable. Here's Oxford and the horticulture station where my high school friends and I joke that UC scientists grow huge cauliflowers in nuked-out soil. I can see Mrs. Forrest's old Victorian on Shattuck near Virginia. She owns the music shop down the street, but Monsieur LeRoux—first oboe in the San Francisco Symphony—has arranged to give lessons in the living room of her home, which he prefers to the cacophonous rooms in the music store. I hobble along the sidewalk, stumping like Chester from *Gunsmoke*, afraid I'll be late. At the top of the steps, Monsieur LeRoux greets me kindly and offers me a café au lait, which he makes on Mrs. Forrest's gas stove. We work on breath control, and he demonstrates again how to fill the diaphragm with air and release it slowly, aspirating so carefully the flame of a candle hardly flickers and will not blow out. All this time, my foot is throbbing.

After the lesson, waiting for the bus by the drugstore on University Avenue, I finally slip off my shoe and examine my foot. The bone juts beneath the skin, bruised and knobby. Tears spring to my eyes. I consider calling home, but that would mean using some of my bus money, and if Mom refuses to come, I'll have to walk back up the hill. As it is, I hoof the usual half hour from the bus stop at Grizzly Peak and Shasta Road. When I get home, dusk has fallen. From the street, the steps are shadowy because no one's turned on the porch light. Is Mom still mad? She seems calm when I find her in the kitchen preparing a chicken, but her eyes darken when I show her my foot. "Why didn't you call me?" she asks. "I'm sure that's broken."

Unbroken

I'm not sure where Dad dredged up the money to buy my older sister
her first horse, a mottled Morab, a three-year-old filly named Gray Lady.
My parents learned about the horse from Wren's riding teacher at Grizzly
Stables. "She's near Martinez," he told us, "in Pacheco Canyon." One
Sunday afternoon we headed out that way, along Alhambra Boulevard.

In the muddy paddock Lady stood, tossing her head and snorting.
The canyon oaks had shed some of their leaves—crenelated forms
that littered the ground. In the dampness, I could detect the scent of
molasses and hay, horehound and thistle. Above the canyon, ragged
clouds drifted in a cold, blue sky. Barely saddle-broken, Lady was a
lovely handful; her owner rode her using a faded blue surcingle and a
hackamore. She responded to the man's weight, his touch, his particular
smell of sweat, faded denim, and worn leather boots.

That day, my younger sister, Laurel, and I crowded near my mom, who
tentatively held pieces of apple to the horse on the flat of her hand.
Wren, fifteen in September, sat astride the young mare and, bright-
eyed, smiling, watched Dad write a check to complete the transaction.
For the next years, Wren trained herself and Lady, remounting after
each accident—a hoof-shaped bruise to her belly, a ripped upper lip,
cracked ribs. I remember her first felt hat, the color of melted chocolate,
her first belt buckle, showing a painted Appaloosa in relief, and her
handsome first saddle with its rawhide seat and tooled leather, custom-
made by a guy in East Oakland.

Then she discovered her first cowboy, Dennis, who, because of a brain fever in childhood, had never learned to read, though he played a mean game of chess. He was slim and long-waisted, wore Wranglers and a tattered red mackinaw with a fake sheepskin lining. He pitched hay and manure, tending the horses for $1.25 an hour at the barn where Lady was stabled. Dennis could have been part Indian, like us, with his black hair and deep brown eyes. He could ride that green horse better than anyone. Mama fell in love with him too, said he reminded her of her favorite brother, and invited the stray young man to live with us in our rambling Berkeley home.

One spring—this was much later—he pushed Laurel down in the corner of a stall at the racetrack, where he and the girls had been hot-walking thoroughbreds, and when she wouldn't stop screaming, Wren came running with a shovel. Struggling with the cowboy's lunging drunkenness, she whacked him on the back until he stumbled away. That was the end of that particular romance with the wild and unruly. The accusations my mom threw at Wren—"cheap" and "chippy"— subsided, and my older sister changed her life. Dad sent Dennis packing, and after that, no more pearl-buttoned shirts to iron. No horses, either—for awhile. My parents shipped Lady up to a farm in Oregon, where she was still high-strung, but finally, over time, grew sedate and wise, though she always had a mind of her own.

New Year's Day

Piled in the car on the way home from the coast,
my family is ruddy with cold,
noses dripping, eyes tearing from the wind.
Rain comes pounding out of charred clouds,
slaps the roof of the car.

We pass through Point Reyes farmland,
the dairy operations, Holsteins with muddy legs,
bellies, and udders. Cows stand in sodden pastures
that will not dry till August.

Meanwhile rain runs in rivulets down slick paths,
soaks into the roots of beach grass and lupine,
beneath the stalks of dead thistle.

Farther inland, creeks take the color of powdery chocolate
and churn between banks that shine with red clay.

My sisters joke and sing carols while we take roads
where mists tangle in boughs of apple trees
planted years ago by Italian farmers.
The smell of damp clothing rises from caps and jackets.

Brother-in-law opens a box of crackers,
cups of hot tea are poured from a thermos,
and the backseat windows steam with music and chatter.

Wedged in the front seat between Dad and me, Mama
takes my hand, taps it against her knee,
keeping time to their voices.

I marvel at how small she's become,
her warm body, her laughter.
Next month, she'll discover
the cancer.

We're all grown now. At last
she's at peace with her daughters.

XXI Century Villanelle

For Sasha Bella Lyric

Because I hear the voices of the dead
at night (who call out in the circling storm),
I cannot cut the knot or loose the thread.

Earth opens; I see a faint trail ahead
but stay among the ones who laugh or mourn.
Because I hear the voices of the dead,

I smudge the air with sage, incense, and red
cedar and pray to see it all transform.
I cannot cut the knot or loose the thread—

and notice now as filaments of web
are woven from my heart, each strand not torn
but whole and bright. The voices of the dead

may sing, while others cry and moan. Instead,
I love the next creations, still unborn,
who cannot cut the knot or loose the thread

and weave their dreams guilelessly, without dread.
How beautiful their thoughts, their lack of scorn!
Because I hear the voices of the dead,
I cannot cut the knot or loose the thread.

Our Mother's Death

A long vigil in the dim room,
the blue curtains drawn at night.
All of us dozed on the hardwood floor
or leaned against a wall in numb wakefulness,
listening.

We knew death was prowling,
perhaps among the trees and downed limbs
behind our house.

It rapped at the windows, then
stood in the room, attentively waiting. Three days,
a little more. Finally the moment came

to escort her—mid-afternoon, gray like any other
with its filter of fog blowing through the grass
on the hill.

Bereft, afraid, we held her upright
till her last breath spiked
and guttered out, like
a person drowning,

                and it lifted her
away from the hot mass

of flesh and nerve that still was
our mother. She was gone,

‚though some reluctance remained
in the cooling air.

Eventually it turned, as we all might,
into something less than air,
more than light.

Dear Soul

I find a few words you scratched
on blue-lined paper, ink fading over time,
a photo of you as a child, frowning
as you hold a blanket to your naked breast.

I remember everything you said—
not each word, but enough
to know your goodness, your resolve.

Where have you gone, dear soul?
Have you learned to value the luster of
your own bright heart? Always I wonder
which star you have become.

Have you joined the flight of birds?
Are you in sunlight shining through
the green of June? Or are you in the wind,
a chime tolling its one true note?

It Was Raining

Wind

What can I say about someone who
touches my bare feet gently,
then fingers the curly down
on my legs and arms,
and finally ruffles the hair
at the crown of my head,
a gesture I'd never let
another try—but wind,
she's okay.

She whispers
a little in my left ear,
the right one, brushes
my upper lip. Then
she sends a cloud
to give me a chill.

She's up there somewhere,
performing interesting magic,
enticing the elements
to come together—
the hydrogen twins
with the oxygen girl,
maybe even getting
a flicker of electricity

out of the thunderheads
gathering to the south,
hoping they'll spark a fire.

The freest soul I know,
she can shove us around
or caress us in the most
unusual ways. She is
certainly exciting, but
what do I really know
about wind?

Stones

Cold and pensive, you make
a habit of silence. Yet
in extremity—earthquake,
avalanche—you call out
in a jumble of voices,
amplified by cliffs
                    and the plummeting fall.

Cautious, shifting slowly,
you cherish the sedentary.
Congregating in fields
and on riverbanks, you sleep
promiscuously, content to be
with others of your kind—roughened,
rounded, or flat.

In your dense, quiet lives
you are admirably stoic
and remote. When shattered,
you try to preserve your dignity
and resist unearthing, yet yield
graciously, generously
to the inevitable dust.

Clouds

Shape-shifters and travelers,
you often journey en masse. In one day
or one night, you cover great distances, moving
and changing, disappearing forever.

You like that circus life,
the acrobatics of choosing what to become: a dog,
an elephant, a leaping porpoise. You accept
the ways in which the wind builds you up,
then breaks you down
until you are wisps,
smears,
ragged wings.

Torn or solitary,
you become mist or fog, hovering in canyons,
drifting in ravines,
indistinct
even to yourselves.

At your most annihilated,
you find yourselves gathering again,
piling up like husks of bark
or a heap of rabbit skins.

You take on faith that heat or cold,
wind or water will bring you together
or tear you apart.

Creek

Beneath the thump
and cascade of water,
under the gulp and pound
where rocks get worn down,
ancestors are singing,
those who were here
so long ago our memory of them
is only music.

You protect these old ones,
disguising their chorus
with your own drumming,
a sound like faint applause.
You give the singers caverns
for their melodies, passages
and pools for their slow
reverberations. At times
we hear laughter, lament,
voices calling,
for the ceremonies
have existed since the first sun
ascended.

Somewhere

beneath your depths

they live, they continue—

unseen, unknown, except

by the ouzel

darting between rocks,

by the kingfisher

swooping along your surface,

or by the river otters,

who bark and dance

to the mysterious tunes.

Cannery, Hood River

We stood for hours by our machines
as the Bartletts jostled by, timed our movements
to the rhythm of the steel peelers,

feeding the cups that grabbed the pears—
six at a time—clamped them tight,
skinned, slit, and sent them to the next

group of women, who sorted the halves
from the bits and quarters, trimmed the pieces
of excess hide. Overhead, cans rattled,

while on the floor, the Hysters maneuvered
back and forth. Our hands, chapped from the troughs
of water, cramped around paring knives.

When the noon whistle blew, we broke
for lunch in the company cafeteria,
sat at square tables, downed our chili,

swilled black coffee, and complained about men,
work, our pitiful pay for which we were grateful,
nonetheless. On days it didn't rain,

my friends and I escaped to the grassy slope
near the county library, ate stolen apples,
dozed in the Indian Summer sun,

listened to tugs on the Columbia pushing
their freight of logs or grain, and sometimes
a sailboat slipped past, tacking down the river

to the Pacific. I felt the pull of the current,
and curiosity welled in me about what
lay beyond where I could see—narrow bridge,

mill yard, railroad tracks that curved east
behind the carved and scoured bluffs. But
when the blast of the signal came at one,

we'd return to work, don hairnets, aprons,
and make haste to our peelers at the back brick wall.
Against the whir of engines, clanking cans, and din of machines,

we'd wait for night, a ride, a six-pack—
each of us guarding unfulfilled dreams.

Near Mosier, Oregon

1

My bed's where the tack gets stored—
saddles and hackamores,
curry combs and bits.
The good scent of horse sweat,
wool, and leather
pervades my dreams.

Nights I can't sleep,
I look out the window
at the span of heaven,
the amber light of stars
that glow in the blackest sky,

or turn the dial on the Bakelite radio,
pick up a wavering signal
from Salt Lake across the plains,
or from San Francisco
down the coast,
over the Cascade range.

A blur of voices—
barking preacher,
sober newsman,
the slick auctioneer—all
mix with the cadence
of country swing.

But when the wind rises
and stirs the boughs
of the canyon oak
outside my window,
I tune to finer things:
rustle of leaves,
winking pulse of stars,
the shape of the wind.

2

Summer and there's hay to mow
and bale in various fields—twelve acres
here, six in Hood River.

I buy new work boots in The Dalles
after my dude boots give out: three weeks
of walking every field each day, dragging
and stacking the bales with hay hooks
for later transport to the barn.

The old lady up the hill jokes that
I want to be "Jon" not "Jan" because I don't
do girly things—but would rather drive the tractor,
learn to ride, throw a rope,
and roll my own smokes.

The two dogs are my friends, Tip and Jack,
and the barn cat, who has no name.

I'm a little in love with my boss's wife.
She's pretty and sweet.

Often I lie at the canyon's edge,
dreaming, looking over the bluff at the old defunct highway
full of rubble, watching a train or the river go by,

hoping no one close to me will know
how much I want to die.

3

I don't actually want to die.
Do I have a right to live?
It's been hammered into me
that I'll be spurned
by a "real woman,"
the only kind I like;
that I'll end up in some bar,
a drunk, old and cynical
before my time.
I'll never find a place
to work, will never be accepted,
I'm told, as long as I refuse
to curl my hair,

thin my eyebrows,
or shave my legs.
There's no place for me
unless I renounce
my crazy longings,
my willful, selfish ways,
the dictates of my own
benighted heart.

Near Mosier

Another Morning

This morning the half-ton Holstein, heavy with calf, barrels through the
barn door and lumbers into her stanchion. Fearless, I squat near her
on the T-shaped milking stool, made with scraps of 2x4. I rub flecks of
dirt from her udders, lean into her warm flank, and massage down the
creamy milk, aiming the stream into a steel bucket I've placed beneath
her. Suddenly I'm hungry. Back in the house, the boss's wife is cooking
hotcakes and bacon; a fresh pot of coffee is percolating. Walking to the
barn not ten minutes ago, I could see the Union Pacific as it rounded
a curve on the Washington side of the Columbia, its headlight flaring
into the river's recesses and across our Oregon hills. The first striations
of morning light were shooting through the clouds on the horizon—
glowing magenta, fiery yellow—turning the sky salmon-colored and
luminous. Sunrise arches over the far hills in Klickitat County, filtering
through the open window of the barn. The pungent scent of tarweed
rises from the pasture, mixing with the far-off smell of pine, scrub
oak, and upturned loam. The Holstein shifts her weight; she sighs as
I pull down the tepid milk. My hands are stronger now than when
I first came to work here in the spring; my fingers no longer ache
from this daily task that takes a full quarter hour. The cat is suddenly
nudging my elbow, awakened from her perch on the highest bale in
the hayloft. I've checked for rattlers in the dim light—nary a one—
and consider how I haven't yet lost a bucket of milk, or my balance,
to the cow's hind leg. As always, wind blows at the lava-edged rim
of the gorge where pale camas flowers poke through thin soil—and

hundreds of feet below the cliffs the semi trucks steam eastward on the interstate. I'm comfortable wearing someone else's shirts and pants, hand-me-downs from my employer, and a pair of Tony Lama boots I've saved up to buy, sturdy enough for this farm work. I don't know my destiny, and I don't know how to love anyone or how to be loved. I'm undeserving. Out there, no one knows this. I could be smart or stupid, but I don't believe I can be anything I want. So I give myself wholly to the moment, to the trees, the cool wind, the harsh bluffs, and to the copper-colored river glinting with light and shadows, blue and silver.

It Was Raining

It was raining,
it was autumn,
a girl was in my arms.

Perhaps to the east
the moon rose
over the crest of the mountains;

to the south
a procession of ghosts came
swinging their censors of iron,

and somewhere a prickly pear
thrust forth its limb of thorns,
a lizard dashed under a rock.

But here it was raining,
a girl was in my arms,
and her skin was fragrant as wheat.

Perhaps in the valley a flock
of night herons settled in oaks
and the bittern heard their hoarse cries;

on the coast a wave

tossed a glass float on the beach

and only a starfish noticed.

But here it was raining,

it was autumn,

the girl's eyes were gray and laughing.

Somewhere a bell kept tolling,

a mother called her child,

and the child was singing;

in the universe a meteor was falling,

the wind stopped suddenly,

an ice crystal was forming.

But here the apples had ripened,

symphonies were playing,

and a girl smiled as she kissed me.

My heart was fiery, but scared

and breaking, for it was autumn

and raining,

         raining,

             raining.

Injun Car

The woman is probably in her mid-thirties. When she calls, her voice is hoarse and agitated, and no sooner than I say *Hello*, she informs me in a rush, "That car you sold me broke down."

I'm standing in the vestibule of my family home, about to sit down to dinner. Everyone has assembled in the dining room, where the meal—a big pan of lasagna—is steaming. My dad is holding up a serving spoon and looking at me inquisitively.

"It was an old car," I answer, hesitantly.

"I have no money to fix that thing," declares the woman, her voice rising. "I can't even have it towed. Will you give me back my hundred dollars?"

"Oh," I stall. "Gosh." I remember how quickly it had happened. She and a lanky blond guy looked under the hood; then they both climbed in the station wagon, with her behind the wheel. They were gone a few minutes, driving around her neighborhood by Mary Magdalene Church, testing the car.

I was surprised at her disheveled appearance. Her forehead was creased, her dark hair looked uncombed. I wondered if the blond was her lover. When she finished driving the car, she handed me two fifty-dollar bills, and I gave her the pink slip.

"I didn't know it would break down," I stammer. "I'm sorry."

It has been three days since the woman called in response to the ad I placed in the *PennySaver*, which read, "1972 Datsun Station Wagon for sale. Still runs. $100 OBO." I had explained on the phone that the twelve-year-old car had a lot of miles on it, that I was selling it "as is."

"My sister drove the car down from Alaska," I had told her. "And she bought it secondhand up there. It's had a long life," I warned. "But it's still kicking."

The next afternoon, I drove the Datsun to the woman's place on Rose Street so she could see if she wanted it.

Though a bit battered, the station wagon's turquoise paint job had held up and could be detected under the rust and dust. Because of its color, we called it the Injun Car. Shortly after my sister Wren returned to California, she and I took the Injun up into the Sierra to go camping. Wren treated that vehicle like a Jeep, taking it over rough back roads, through creek beds and muddy washes. We found a Forest Service road that led to a small meadow surrounded by ponderosa pine and sagebrush at the edge of nowhere. We made a campsite, heated up some beans on the Coleman stove, and built a small fire to keep warm. Soon the stars came out; the night got chilly. When we ran out of stories, we let the fire burn down and rolled out our sleeping bags.

"It isn't fair to keep my money," the woman is saying. Her voice is louder; she's beginning to cry. "The car is broken. I'm stuck here in this town. Please!"

Months after our camping trip, Wren gave the vehicle to me. She had commuted in it for two semesters, back and forth from our home in the Berkeley Hills to Cal State, Hayward, where she was studying ornithology. My sister kept her gear in the back, charred cooking pots, the cookstove, a sleeping bag, hiking boots, some field guides, and a tattered Mexican blanket she had found in the desert. I inherited some of this stuff when she gave me the car. Meanwhile, Wren had acquired a new man. He was a sweet, quiet guy who drove a long, white Ford sedan with a red interior. It had been his family's car; he called it White Fang.

"Wait a minute," I tell her.

"What is it?" Dad calls across the table.

I put my hand over the receiver.

"The lady I sold the Datsun to. She wants her money back."

Dad says nothing for a moment. "Tell her you've already spent it."

I consider this. The bills she paid me are still in my wallet, but I am saving this money to buy a Martin mandolin. With the sale of the Injun Car, I have just enough to go to The Fifth String tomorrow and purchase that instrument. Telling the lady I've already spent the money is a lie, but I've wanted that sweet-sounding mandolin a long time.

"Listen," I tell the woman, "I can't give that money back. It's not mine anymore. It's gone, spent."

I hear her take this in. "Oh," she cries. She is sobbing. "But you sold me a piece of junk. It's a rotten car!"

"I'm really sorry." I do feel contrite. "I told you that it had a lot of miles. But," I reason, "that Datsun was still running when you bought it. You drove it. You decided. It's not my fault that the car broke down. And now the money you paid me is gone. I'm sorry."

Her tears stop. She's sniffling. I hear her draw in her breath. She's silent a moment. I fidget, anxious for the conversation to end. My family has begun eating supper. I can hear them discussing the Injun Car. Wren is laughing about the number of times she ran out of gas because the gauge didn't work.

Suddenly the woman snaps, "You cheated me! It's not fair!" And she slams the receiver into its cradle.

I feel terrible. Who was to know that the car would die so soon after changing hands? I loved that car, had driven it all kinds of places where, it's true, it had run out of gas and had even gone kaput so that my dad had to come tow me using our old pickup truck. On rainy days last fall I had held my girlfriend in my arms in that Injun Car and had kissed her passionately. It was a great car, a turquoise gem.

The Window

In early October the open
window of your office
lets in Indian summer's
rustle of oak leaves,
gusts of east wind.

On the shady path below,
through Berkeley's campus,
other students walk, hurrying
to an afternoon class
at the foot of Wheeler Hall.
But I am all heartbeat
and inner whispers as you,
head bent, silent,
read my ode of love.

At your desk, you lean forward,
one hand at your temple,
one hand trembling
the paper. Your quick
eyes glisten as you scan my words.

When you come round to where I sit
watching in a straight-back chair,
your body's fragrance

reminds me of bread,

sun, and lemons. I lick my lips,

beckon my breath, and look

at your thin waist,

slender hips, your flushed face.

The clock in your office

ticks, the Campanile chimes

the mid-hour. Outside,

a Stellar's jay calls

from a hedge of lilacs, fog

gathers near the Farallones.

The scent of dust and eucalyptus

drifts through the window

like a wish. You bend down and kiss

the crown of my head,

my black hair.

Field Guide

Trillium along the trail we know,
but other flowers we do not.
So we go into a nature store at
the top of the muddy path
and pore over a field guide,
side by side, as close
as it is good, laughing
and asking, "Five petals or four?
Long stem or short?"

Standing near you, I am like
an adolescent. I find a toy bear,
place his muzzle against your neck.
He wants to kiss you sweetly. He likes
the scent of your skin, says it is better
than almost any flower.

On our walk we hardly touch
but for the strong hug
in the rain-soaked meadow
near the blossoming tree.
And then the softer embrace
on the wooden bridge. We watch
the clear stream trickle down
among the ferns and salal

after stooping to peer at the unusual

red snail who paused

to let us admire her on her journey

across the wet footpath.

Portland

My shoes are soaked,
my skin is damp.
I like the smell of wet wool
after we've stood in the rain
trying to jump-start your car.
Water collects at my hairline.
I feel it beading on my forehead,
a band of watery light.
I'm made clean by it
and hopeful.
It's hard not to smile,
even though you'll pay dearly
for a new battery or starter
and we're running late for class, for work.

But slowed down, I notice
the swirling sky, how the dark
branches of the trees drip with condensation,
how the red leaves of the vine maple blow bravely
over the asphalt.

Later we'll talk politics
and sit laughing with friends,
drinking coffee and feeling rich
in this stretch of poverty.

The sleeves of my coat
are almost dry. I feel
the faint touch of pearls
and diamonds threaded among
the roots of my hair.

A Gift from My Students

My students, Minh and Hoa,
sit across from me
in the little restaurant on Sandy Boulevard,
where Minh works weekends.
It is evening, after our last class
at the community college,
and I am their guest.
They confer quietly in Vietnamese,
suggest a salad of papaya and shrimp,
or Canh Chua Ga—chicken soup
with tomatoes and pineapple.
"It is very good," says Minh.
I smile while they press me
to select several things—
seafood with lemon grass,
grilled beef with crushed peanuts,
noodles and rice.

"In our country," says Hoa,
"we celebrate national Teacher's Day.
Teachers are given a day off
and their pupils come to their houses
to thank them."

I imagine the streets alive with students
marching in groups, laden with small gifts
of food, books, sheaves of paper trimmed in gold leaf,
poems they have written. Everywhere
in that mild country
the learners are laughing and talking,
standing shyly and excitedly
at their teachers' doors.

Lovely scholars, you are earnest
and study hard. You do not despise
the ones who tutor you.
No one has told you
how utterly expendable I am.

But tonight we celebrate, tell stories,
savor the sweet and sour.

Six Sonnets

Crossing the West

1

Desert heat, high clouds, and sky
the color of lapis. On this journey,
anything seems possible,
so we stop by an ancient cottonwood
to kiss. The beauty trembles,
doesn't say a word, just watches
me, so open. Small birds fly by, flock
in the shady tree above us. What
settles in her heart? What congeals?
Hope? Despair? Far off, the river churns
in its sandy banks, swallows veer, turn
in fiery air. Will these kisses seal
her to me? I her lover, she my wife?
Is all of this a dream, my whole life?

2

She is just this side of wonderful,
and suddenly the glamorous world
fills itself with shining and we laugh
at highway monuments that explain
how hard the trek had been for Franciscans
in the Indian wilderness, poor fellows—
conversion is the devil's own
work! Then the stones of her dream

turn up under her feet, the back
of a huge land turtle. I know
we must be circling Paradise
because the ants enter the fleshy petals
of the roadside flowers with evident
joy and purpose (oh, my dark, pretty one).

3

Music, my adored. When is there never
music? My accordion puffs up
with drinkable melodies. I spill
her tunes into your listening ear,
one after the other: the squeeze-box
enters the dance of the plaintive gypsy
with its hard rhythms, lilts the back-
breaking labor song the worker croons
to earth, warbles romantic notes of
dissolving borders. You melt
like a woman beneath her lover's touch.
Music is happy and pitiless when
it sets fire to combustible souls. Even
the raspy bandoneon's voice is lyric.

4

Sacred. Sacred. Sacred. Sacred. (Speak
in a whisper.) We slip into this
space half cognizant. The land is very
large indeed: bones of the earth
worn down, though she is a living thing.

See how she exposes her grace? Antelopes
graze on the far plain—their high,
white tails—the red soil throbs
its slow heartbeat, and the blue sky
clears so smartly, perfectly, like
radiance. Are the ancestors near?
What can we know? We decide
to wander around this prairie, mistaken
for Utes, buy commodities in little towns.

5

Late afternoon we head west along the willow-banked
Malheur after the long curve of the Snake River plain.
(Above the falls where the Shoshone went to pray
we soaked our feet in cold water, and I observed
the arch of her brown foot.) Rabbitbrush and sage
along the highway, juniper on far hills and bluffs.
Sundown, and dusk falls over the wide basin of land.
In Burns we eat eggs in a cafe, take a room
in the Motel 6. In the dark, I can see
her black hair, black against the pillows. Its clean
scent makes me think of corn. At dawn, I hold her
and there are kisses. Then more kisses. Then more.
The day is cold; a north wind blew last night. But
the land is open. Rain falls in showers of light.

6

Her hand on my thigh, my shoulder,
in my hair. She leans over to kiss my cheek.

We look at each other, smile. For miles
we travel this way, nearly silent, point
with eyes or chins at the circling hawk, the king-
fisher on the snag above the swollen
creek. One night I weep in her arms
as she cries, "Oh, oh, oh!" because I have touched
her scars lightly: throat, belly, breasts.
In that communion of lovers, thick sobs
break from me as I think of my love
back home, all that I have done
and cannot say. This is the first time
I have left her so completely, so alone.

Poema de amor

Spent the night in Mojave

at the edge of the desert

one cold January on my way

home to you. At dawn,

I filled the tank at an Arco, bought

a steamy cup of java, then

got on the road, driving east,

alone. The radio waves were full of static

in that old Ford Falcon till I hit

la emisión mexicana

and a two-tone accordion

waltzed over the wires,

a duet of voices,

and that lovely, rapid-fire

Spanish blasting up

from across the border,

and suddenly there were

straw hats and roses,

pan dulce, La Virgen

de Guadalupe, thick ristras

of chiles, crimson,

gloriously hot. The sun

crept over the horizon,

a streak of cochineal,

and a chilly fog

drifted in gullies,

socked itself in along

the Colorado. How I wanted

to be in your arms. While rain

plummeted down in Kingman

at the base of Hualapai Mountain,

snow came falling

like tiny feathers all around

Flagstaff, the peaks

of San Francisco.

I'd planned to stay

in the high country,

but now I kept driving

out of the white drifts

and into the desert.

Navajo and Hopi lay

to the north, Winslow

and Holbrook to the east—

miles of red bluffs

and dark mesas,

cliffs the color of ocher,

ancient seabed of shells

and bones. By the time I reached

Gallup, it was a matter of

hours till I saw the Rio Grande.
Night had descended.
I could sense the presence
of mountains; the wind
buffeted the creaking car. Sudden
gusts of snow dusted
the windshield. Still
stars glittered in a black,
cloudless sky. Up ahead
were the lights of Albuquerque,
the sandy shores of the river,
and you in our first apartment
down near the bosque—
how you'd smile to see me,
how you'd laugh—oh!

I missed the fields and
pastures of the North Valley,
the crumbling adobes,
irrigation ditches,
scent of piñón.
I thought of the names
of those staunch families—Lovato,
Griegos, Candelaria,
Montaño—and of you,
my dear hispana,

your sweet hips

and warm hugs—mi corazón,

mi bien-amada—

what we whispered

when we made love.

Owl

I have decided to befriend the night
and the blank, cotton-mouthed sleeplessness
that claims my spirit.

I am anywhere the half-moon sails,
its ghost-light breaking through clouds
in the salty, windswept sky. Like owl,

I float over shadowed walls
and fences, the nocturnal alleys
of backyard blossoms—hollyhock,

blackberry, wild anise. In the deep thicket
of pines that grows in the creek bed
behind the house, I perch,

or among blue leaves of the eucalyptus
that click in the breeze while its cool,
oily fragrance lifts into the dark.

I try out my voice, send forth
its husky syllable into night-stained streets
and rain-washed boulevards in cities

where the poor sleep, bunched up

against the cold in doorways,

their breath of tar and acids.

Navigating black currents of air,

unseen, unremarked, I understand

the giddy pleasure of darkness,

the uncanny moment of calling

into the pitch of morning. These wings

take me anywhere. Over shuttered houses

I glide, my voice stuttering—

an energetic harpy, a rasping entity

of unappeasable appetite.

Dawn

Before the earliest birds sweep through the yard,
light a candle. Ask this day for refuge,
music, and poems,

for sunlight warming the walls,
for the animal self at peace.

Ask to know the path into vibrant stillness.

Give thanks for humble foods—
the leavened and unleavened breads.

Praise the sun edging the horizon,
the dove-colored sky, washed clean.

Good Luck

My sister hands me a horseshoe.
"Here," she says, "for good luck."

We have hiked into that part of the mountains
where the quaking aspen grows—white,

slender groves whose fallen bark curls
like the edges of old maps.

In the shadow of those trees,
air is dank, the meadow still wet

from snowmelt or a summer shower.
Water seeps under fallen branches,

and the sweet smell of wild iris
fills the air, faint violet spears

in the short, sparse grass. We can just see the lake—
it reflects the sky, deep turquoise,

silver, and black. I think the water must be
cold, but on the trail where packhorses trod,

the mud is warm. Mosquitoes will hatch
in the molecules of sticky earth and grass. No clock

but nature in these New Mexican highlands,
in land pirated from the Indians long ago.

The clouds drifting over the far ridge
remind me of a pile of clean linens,

and I can hear a rumble of thunder,
but my sister only whistles for her dog,

who has found the rotten carcass
of a half-eaten elk and rolls

with lolling tongue,
then dashes into the timber.

"She's riding in the back of the truck,"
laughs my sister, and we walk on

in the bright sun. On our trail, veins of
quartz and schist break through the soil,

and I feel the peculiar weight of iron
in my hand, my sister's gift—

the sheen on the lake, the smell of mud,
the rusty metal flaking beneath my thumb.

Tucson

Winter in this landscape: dry wind,
dry clouds, dry snow on the highest peaks.
Chilly mornings. The mountains, striated,
marked by planetary upheavals.

Land of skeletons and shades.
Land of buried water and plants
that grow crooked and spiny.

In this place I work
to keep my roots wet, find joy
in this winter dawn—cold yellow
warming to gold.

I walk out to watch:
Wind picks up, dies down,
then returns hard,
sending spirals of leaves
across the shallow river bed.

Birds scatter as I approach,
their wings lifted by the wind.

A year ago Dad passed away,
a ravaging death, leaving us
lonelier than before.

The sky brightens to the color of
Mexican morning glories that straggle
over backyard fences. Daybreak
finds me shivering,
talking myself into hope.

Winter solstice. They say we cannot know
what lies ahead. I feel I am being born,
borne, not refused.

Somnabulista

A thin voice calls and you rise,
helpless, and go out through the door
into a city of mists. You wander
through plazas and mazes,
into parks and over bridges,
past cafés and pastelerías.
You drift down alleys,
over rooftops, ignoring the pull of earth,
wearing a cautious smile.

An inconsequent breeze
is the surest guide;
it knows every corner
and precipice, the steepest ways,
those most narrow and rigorous.

Snarling dogs quiet at your approach,
cats leap away. No rat scuttles across your path,
no rabid animal confronts you.
Drowsing birds remain motionless
among twigs and leaves as you pass by.

You can negotiate anything,
now that your touch is light
and your eyes see through this darkness.

You wander among stars and clouds,

doubters and dreamers, certain

children who understand cruelty

but rely on the heart's

unreasoning support.

Notes and Acknowledgments

If the first line of "We Could Not Forget" seems familiar, it's because I lifted it from Luci Tapahonso's poem "In 1864." I used Tapahonso's poem to teach my students the pantoum form, asking them to select a line from her poem that spoke to them. Her line, "The journey began, and the soldiers were all around us" spoke to me. This poem can be found in Luci's book *Sáanii Dahataal: The Women Are Singing*, published by the University of Arizona Press, 1993.

"Tribal History" was originally titled "Bound Poem #2." I wrote it at the University of Arizona's Poetry Center during its October 2007 Housewarming Celebration. The poem is a "found" poem, constructed from a set of provided words under timed conditions. For more information, see http://poetrycenter.arizona.edu/postandbind/gould. shtml. The poem emerged from a hazy memory. Years ago I read Donald P. Jewell's *Indians of the Feather River: Tales and Legends of Concow Maidu of California* (Ballena Press, Menlo Park, 1987) in which the story of the lynching tree is recorded.

"XXI Century Villanelle" was originally published as a limited edition broadside, typeset and printed by Marie-Elise Wheatwind and illustrated by her son, James Woodard. It was included in "April Is the Cruelest Month," a group show of letterpress broadsides in the Basil Hallward Gallery at Powell's City of Books, in Portland, Oregon, spring 2002. The entire portfolio, which benefits Literacy Volunteers, can be found at http://www.powells.com/biblio/1-2221131652375-0.

This book of poems has been many years in the making. I am grateful to the editors at the University of Arizona Press for suggestions on revising this manuscript, and especially to Patti Hartmann for her encouragement.

Several friends also read this manuscript, or parts of it, while it existed in raw form and gave me feedback and advice. I thank Sandy Dorr, Chris Faatz, Lisa Greseth, Andrea Herrera, Rebecca Ruiz Jenab, Julie Kasper, Jane Martin, Paulann Petersen, Becky Thompson, Linda Watts, and Mimi Wheatwind.

I owe a debt of gratitude to my sisters for their support and willingness to let me share family stories.

Thanks, too, to editors of the following publications who published some of these poems, many of them in somewhat different form: News from Native California; Deer Drink the Moon: Poems of Oregon; Bear Flag Republic: Prose Poems and Poetics from California; Spring Salmon, Hurry to Me!; Sentence: A Journal of Prose Poetics; Manzanita Review; Pilgrimage; Three Coyotes; and Native Literatures: Generations.

About the Author

Janice Gould (Concow) grew up in Berkeley, California, attending Laney and Merritt Junior Colleges before entering the University of California, Berkeley, where she majored in linguistics. After graduating with Honors and Distinction in General Scholarship, she continued studying for a master's degree in English at UC, and upon completion, entered the PhD program in English at the University of New Mexico. She was awarded her doctorate from UNM in 2000. In December 2008, Janice completed her master's degree in library science at the University of Arizona (as well as the requirements for certification in museum studies from the Department of Art History). Janice's academic honors include fellowships from the Ford Foundation and the Roothbert Fund, as well as scholarships from the Association of Research Libraries and the University of Arizona's Knowledge River Program.

Janice has published two previous collections of poetry, *Earthquake Weather* (University of Arizona Press, 1996) and *Beneath My Heart* (Firebrand Press, 1990). She has also published a chapbook/artbook titled *Alphabet* (May Day Press, 1966). Janice's scholarly publications (co-edited with Dean Rader) include *Speak to Me Words: Essays on Contemporary American Indian Poetry* (University of Arizona Press, 2003). Janice is the recipient of writing grants from the National Endowment for the Arts and from the Astraea Foundation, a fund for lesbian writers. She is an assistant professor in Women's and Ethnic Studies (WEST) at the University of Colorado in Colorado Springs.

Library of Congress Cataloging-in-Publication Data

Gould, Janice, 1949–

    Doubters and dreamers / Janice Gould.

        p. cm. — (Sun tracks ; v. 67)

    ISBN 978-0-8165-2927-8 (pbk. : acid-free paper)

    1. Indians of North America—Poetry. I. Title.

    PS3557.O862D68 2011

    811'.54—dc22

                            2010021797